"SWAMP WATER, ABALONE SHELLS, BASTED EGGS, SOW BELLY AND NETTLES"

"SWAMP WATER, ABALONE SHELLS, BASTED EGGS, SOW BELLY AND NETTLES"

Memoirs
from the heart of a
Little Big Man

Laguna Beach, California
March 11, 1992

by
Chad Morton Bowlin

Swamp Water, Abalone Shells,
Basted Eggs,
Sow Belly and Nettles:
Memoirs
from the heart of a
Little Big Man
Copyright © 1992
Chad Morton Bowlin.
Produced and printed
by Stillwater River Publications.
All rights reserved. Written and produced in the
United States of America. This book may not be reproduced
or sold in any form without the expressed, written
permission of the author and publisher.
Visit our website at
www.StillwaterPress.com
for more information.
First Stillwater River Publications Edition.
Originally published by Pendejo Productions,
a Division of GTFO, Ltd.,
Laguna Beach, CA..
Library of Congress Control Number: 2021910028
ISBN-13: 978-1-955123-20-4
1 2 3 4 5 6 7 8 9 10
Written by Chadwick Morton Bowlin.
Cartography by Chadwick Morton Bowlin.
Illustrations by Michelle Bowlin.
Published by Stillwater River Publications,
Pawtucket, RI, USA.

*The views and opinions expressed
in this book are solely those of the author
and do not necessarily reflect the views
and opinions of the publisher.*

Map of the Area

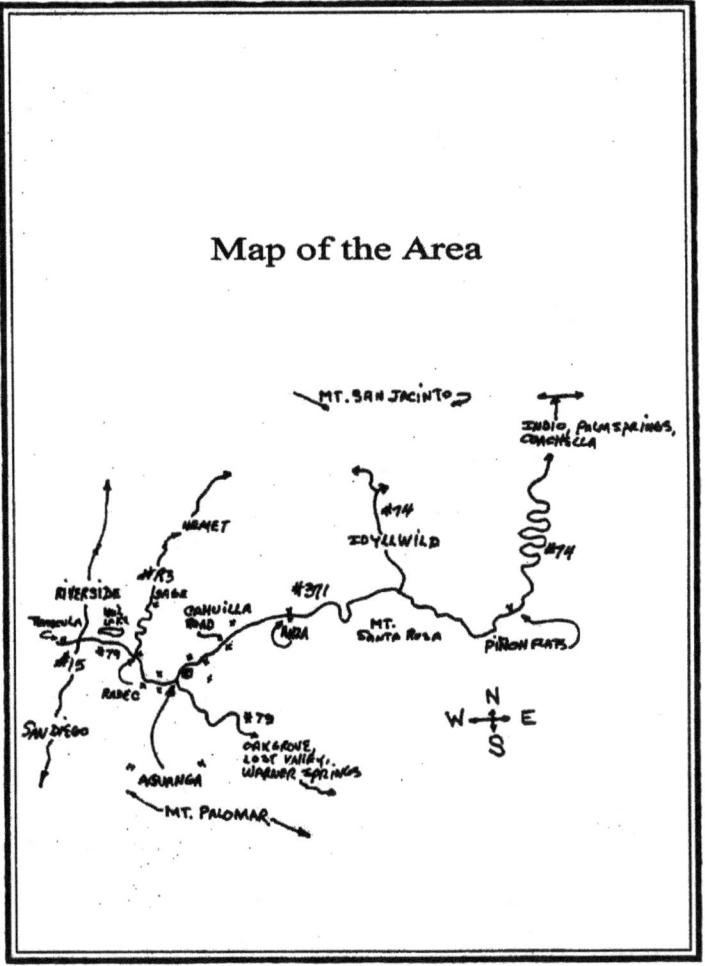

Dedicated to

Friends & Family

and……. **Slatten**

☙ ❧

Contents

Preface 11

Introduction 15

Abalone Shells 21

Swamp Water 29

Tree in the House 39

Gas Reefer 45

Sow Belly & Basted Eggs 53

Mail Route 59

Spooking Mule & Snake 67

Nettles 79

Silent Places 89

Wire of Death 95

Slaughterhouse 103

Cottonwood Reunions 111

Pools 121

Baga's Hash 131

Olla Caves 139

Pinon Flats 147

Isinglass Slide 155

Pines to Palms 165

❧ PREFACE ❧

Several hundred years ago there were Indians and ponies in the Hill Country of Southern California…… in an area between Temecula and Warner Hot Springs. They were peaceful people with existence in the mountainous, temperate, beautiful climate having only to work and prepare for the moons ahead. There were no warring factions or invaders then. It was a joy to live…… and a joy to die. Going to the "Land of the Great White Father" was not something to fear, but a stage in one's life to expect, to speak of, and to celebrate when one was called.

The Spanish came first. Valleys and canyons were turned into places of refuge. Freedom of movement was gone. In the Spanish effort to "colonize and educate the pagans," life as a Cahuilla Indian was over… and with it the right to live, love, languish and laugh with each other. The primary goal now was to stay alive. They became servants to the rich and slaves to each other. Life and independence as they knew it is gone forever.

Then the White Man came. The "Butterfield Stage" came right through here and ended nearby. My relatives helped settle this territory. I am very proud to be a fifth generation Californian. I sat on my Great, Great Grandmother Lucia's lap and I have the pictures to prove it. I am not all proud of the White Man coming. I know where the Red man made his arrowheads and stored his cooking pots and ollas. In respect, I will not tell.

This story is of the Hill Country as I saw it. The Red Man is there today. The "Reservation" is not a home, it is a place to stay. Few of God's Red Children are left. The hills are beautiful, but empty. What can I say?

I can remember and I have. It feels good to remember. It can hurt to forget.

Don't ever say... ***"Good-bye,"*** say ……….. ***"So long."***

CMB

❧ INTRODUCTION ☙

A story not unlike that of your own, but this is mine, something I can really call "my own." Very few things we mortals can truthfully call.... our own. It is from the "formative years," whatever they are, and this is true. Few things we read or hear today are truthfully true.

Motivation to write? Certainly not monetary as anyone can write their story, but it's the gratification of putting to "pen" one's private thoughts.

Memoirs are similar to pictures we take of friends, family, food, faces and folks; nobody really enjoys seeing pictures of other people except the people themselves. Kindness, on occasion, may prevail, but one's own pictures bring instant recognition to the photographer….. same as the printed word to the author.

There still is part of a small boy in a Man where, if he could, he would return, if even for an instant. He would be that Little Man for a short time again, and he would be happy. ***This is what we remember.***

Chadwick Morton Bowlin

Without you Dear Reader, my thoughts would be but a few bytes on recycled paper.

Flashes of life to ponder……… ………… ***and this is where we begin.***

CMB

I

"ABALONE SHELLS"

Standing in the shower looking at the marvelous ideas put to reality by Joe, I drifted and dreamed. I was about 9 and believed everybody, everywhere, about anything, and especially believed….. my Grandfather. His name was Joe….. and he could do no wrong. The year was 1940….. and all folks were just beginning to come out of the deep depression and starting to sell their home grown vegetables to the market down " below."

Abalone Shells

In the shower Joe had made (yes….. he made the WHOLE thing), I was looking at the ABALONE SHELLS imbedded in cement to hold the soap bar. They were flush inside the cement, and Joe's hands (and my hands too) fit well inside the shell in front of the mother of pearl and the soap just fit exactly right….. and the little holes nature made in the shell for the ABALONE, they served as water drain holes for the soapy water to flow away so you didn't get this yucky, messy, goo that soap gets if it sits in water. What a brilliant man my Grandfather! The holes were on the bottom and side and the shell was put in right so the soap drained….. and nature provided the exact perfect fit for the soap bar!! Bath or hand size!!! The shell itself also worked as a handle for my Grandmother and other old people to steady themselves by grasping the shell while soaping with the other hand!

The shower he made was a wonder of the world!! Galvanized 3/4 inch pipe snaked over the roof on the top of the house over the bedroom….. (painted black of course, to absorb the heat of the sun) and we had hot water every evening for showers for everyone!! It's called "Solar Heating" today! You had to be tough to take a shower in the morning! We would all take "submarine showers" where we got wet, turned the hot off and soaped down, turned hot on again and rinsed!! When I was alone and they were gone evenings to hunt deer at night on the alfalfa, I used to just "let er rip" and use it all!! Such good memories. Joe had two head sprays, one mounted above your head like a rain shower, and the other like the conventional pointing at your face, neck, or lower depending on your height! Also, two faucets extra were built into the cement. One you could turn on that sprayed your feet, and the other I never did understand until I traveled Europe 30 years later. When opened up full it sprayed you either in the frontal or rear privates….. depending on the way you wished to face!! There were two small windows open on each side to the world for fresh air and cross ventilation to keep the mildew down. Bugs, dust, and very cold air came in also, but this was tolerated cause it was a good place for the girls to put the shampoo bottles on the little shelves above the water spray. A lot of hair pins and bobby pins ended up on these little shelves too.

Shower floors always seem slippery today ….. and the rubber mats and non-skid stuff on the floor is dark and dirty and needs cleaning. Joe built a walnut floor rack over the drain….. now how simple can you get and still be a genius?? No mildew….. slats were close enough together to catch the soap when it dropped, and not so big that your toes got caught. No body ever stood in water….. it went away under the walnut shower rack clean as a whistle. Every month one of my chores was to take the rack out… hose it down and scrub it and the cement floor… let the rack sit in the hot sun for a day….. and presto, magico….. brand new clean! Clorox and Lux flakes did wonders!!

The SWAMP. Where our source for all the water came from, to create the well water for drinking, and showers and irrigation and for the animals….. and for our POWER to wash clothes!! Joe again. Never could he do wrong... he was gifted and I watched him with great intensity every time he did anything. Pulling on his Bull Durham string with his teeth, lighting his match on the back of his overalls and twisting the hen's neck off with a swirl so it was second only to the master of the baton!! Now to the power. At 9 years old I accepted everything that anyone did that was new and good….. and most all things were new and good at that age!! How do you get power from a SWAMP?? Joe knew and he was about to show me.

II

"SWAMP WATER"

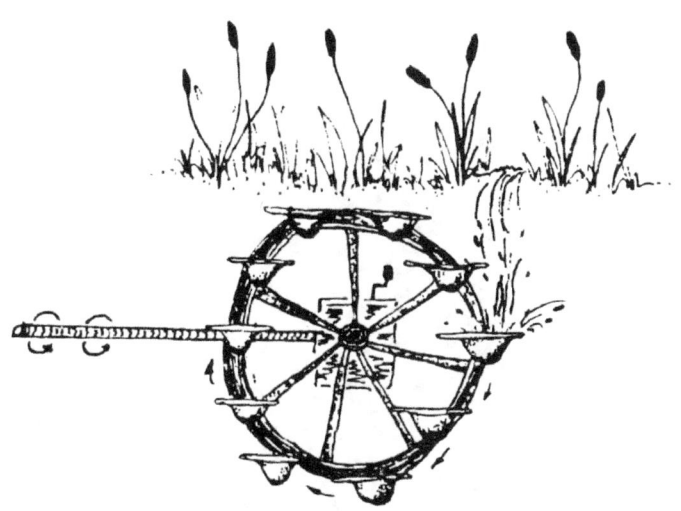

There was a period in my life where we had no electricity. As I recall, the nearest, was some 35 miles away from the electric plant in Hemet, California. But, as a child I didn't really care about that. If I had thought about it, I probably would have not worried about not having electric lights and plugs for vacuum cleaners and hair dryers and clock radios and computers and modems etc., as the "elders" took that to account and it was not for a child to be concerned. After all, I had the same amount of light as anyone, enough light to see at night, and no more or no less than Joe or "Gram," my Grandmother, (God bless her, and I just <u>know</u> <u>He does</u>,….. <u>often</u>). Nevertheless, some things were really tough without having what we never had… like when we would visit "down the hill" and play turning on and off the light switch… yes, it used to be a real switch, that you turned from left to right to turn on, and opposite to turn off. Like the big switches today in terminal boxes, only smaller. They really made a spark, too!! Now we have silent mercury switches, touch pads and noise turner oners by clapping hands or just moving in the room!! Anyway, we had nothing in Aguanga (that's Indian, for water). I'll tell you later where this place is.

Now………

SWAMP WATER POWER. The SWAMP provided irrigation water for the row crops, and water for the stock, and pigs and chickens, ducks, turkeys, etc. But, you could not drink it….. or we just didn't cause it was sort of grayish and just couldn't be good. So, we had a well that was the softest water ever made… this we drank, showered in and pumped in the kitchen sink. So, Joe thought and thought (I guess) and started to build a funny looking contraption. He got some dozen or so coal buckets that looked just like a fireman's hat up-side down, mounted them to a giant 6 to 8 foot wheel that he made from scraps. What he had fixed and laying on the ground for the longest time was a big wheel, with about 12 spokes and a center ring that was made of oak, and the hats mounted to the outside of the wheel at the junction of the spokes.

Swamp Water

He did lots of digging behind the chicken coop, some 30 feet from the metal work shop. He mixed cement and poured it into two wooden structures he had built as a frame for the cement. Then he took an old model A Ford axle which was magically sized to fit very tightly right into the center of the oak Wheel ring, greased it with axle grease, placed in between the now hardened frames. You now had the wheel threaded with the axle, mounted between the concrete pieces….. it was a big wheel, with buckets/hats sticking out toward the swamp above. Unbeknown to me, the Indian hired hand had already channeled the water seeping out of the SWAMP into a little stream that now had running water in it!!

This stream came to the edge of the Swamp some 6-8 feet above the

axle center and created a water fall…..
into the first bucket/hat!! And the wheel
turned!! A water wheel!!! Now I knew
what he had made… and sensing my
joy and curiosity, he sat down and told
me the plans. I was mesmerized with
awe! The next few weeks I "helped"
him build the finished product.

Now that the water wheel was
turning fast, he took the same old Ford
model A and got the transmission out of
it. He and I made a base of scrap wood
to one side of the wheel, put the transmission in it up high, poured the concrete and moved the trans in place to
fasten to the axle that was now turning
greased "U" joint bearings. We meshed
gears and… magic again!! With another junk stick trans (no automatics
then!), he/we took several long pieces
of 3/4" pipe, welded them together in a

Swamp Water

long rod some 25-35 feet long, mounted them on concrete posts with bearing sleeved holes we greased, and meshed to the other transmission. At the other end, Joe took Gram's washing machine and the rubber squeezers (that wrung out clothes when you turned the handle), and somehow took small gears with levers and built them all close together.

Now….. here is what we had. When you put the first trans in low gear, it meshed to the long rod and made it turn, but nothing happened until you put the second transmission in low gear and meshed it to the washer. Presto, the washer blades turned squish/squish/squish. When Gram thought the wash was done, she threw a little lever by the washer trans, and it moved the "power" to the wringer!! And the swamp water made the waterfall, that turned the wheel, that timed the rod, that turned the washer blades, that, (when shifted) wrung the clothes!! Joe never did figure out how to wring and wash at the same time! But, it was the miracle of Aguanga and lasted many, many years. A moment to remember.

III

"TREE IN THE HOUSE"

At this writing, I have in 59 odd years slept with a lot of different types of things, some I wish not to recall, but I am very proud of sleeping in the same room….. with a TREE. Yes, a TREE, not a bush, but an honest to goodness tree. Not a sapling, but a real 5 to 8 foot in diameter trunk that grew right out of the floor 6 feet from my feather bed. Now, we all know that a TREE is not just going to sprout in the floor and grow that big. No, never. But, to Joe it was a challenge. He built the

Tree in the House

little house years before and the TREE was to the side of it, enjoyed as any TREE should be by people sitting under her, eating under her and whatever else good people do, night or day, under a big TREE outside. Secrets only the tree knows. A very valuable source of information if it could speak. Anyway, the house became too little for them (me moving in didn't help). They needed room for guests anyway. So, Joe thought again. "Hell" he said, "the swamp is too close to the left, can't build that way, the back and abalone shower is close to the chicken coup, and you just can't build closer to the road, so expand to the right!." Yes, TREE was there, about 8 feet from the kitchen.

In a few months, TREE was still there, with little petunias growing around the circumference with a little ditch some 8-10 inches all-round it. But the big difference was TREE was inside the house!! If Mohammad won't come to the mountain, the mountain comes to Mohammad!! Joe had built a roof 12-15 feet out from the kitchen, circled the tree (leaving room for rain water to run down to water the petunias and to allow for natural expansion). The roof went some 15 feet to the front and some 30 feet to the back. Screened in, and my feather bed right near the pantry, in front of TREE. What better place for a young man to sleep? Protected from the elements by a TREE and open to the world. In the winter time JOE had canvas flaps that came down over the screens to keep some of the cold outside, and my feather bed kept me warm. More about the pantry later. And, the Servel gas refrigerator. A time to reflect.

IV

"GAS REEFER"

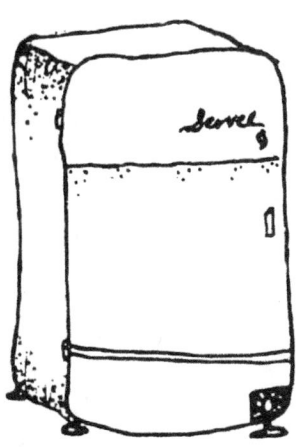

A little flame that made an, oh-so very quiet noise... that could only be heard in the dead of night... after all living things such as birds, crickets and everything were asleep. Except me and the little gas flame that seemed to sort of hiss... very, very quietly. As I lay on my feather bed in the screened in room, I would listen, and listen. When I heard the little gas flame purr... I knew then that all the world was napping... every thing, any where in the world for sure..... it just had to be! I saw the dim

Gas Reefer

light under the GAS REEFER flicker and purr. I would lay awake for hours wondering how a little gas flame that purred could keep everything cold?? The name on the GAS REEFER said "Servel" and the logo-insignia was a blue flame about one inch long. No explanation as to how it worked. I would drift off to sleep with that last thought….. how could it be?

For many years the Ice man came every three days to put ice in the Ice Box. I have good thoughts of this happening, as he would, on special occasion (what determined this I do not know) give me a popsicle. It seemed each time a different flavor. And it seemed it was always a hot day when he came, never on a cold day. Never could understand this either. The ice box was now a cupboard that held things that would not fit anywhere else, with a plant on the top. It was just a box that had a sort-of metal door with a shiny chrome handle that you pulled on to open it. Today these pieces are prized bits of furniture with all the oak wood polished like it never was before. Strange how things change, isn't it?

Next to the REEFER was the pantry. Now, if you have never had a pantry, you haven't lived!! This is the dark room where all the stuff Gram "put up" was stored. I can taste the strawberry jam now… full of seeds and lumps of strawberry meat that just exploded in your mouth!! Especially when it was smeared on a piece of home baked, salt rising bread, with peanut butter!!! I used to push the paraffin top away a little bit and taste the new flavors she had tried. Flavors like fresh apricot and fresh from the tree, tangerine marmalade! I tried to put the paraffin top back on exactly like it was……….. but I'm sure she knew what I had done. She always did. There was fresh "canned" corn, beans, beets (ugh!), cucumbers, peaches and all sorts of things. In the winter this is where she got most of the food for our meals. There were even "canned" meats like beef and pork and pickled pigs feet. I never figured out why they called it "canning" when everything was in a Ball or Kerr jar! The pantry had its own special smells too!

Great courage was mustered to ask Joe a question. For to do so, I had to be ready to take a "Why?," or much more difficult, a "sit down and I will tell you." And the time it took was a marvel. He knew everything, about anything, at anytime, about anyplace, anywhere! Yes, I did it. I asked Joe, "How does a little flame keep ice cream and milk cold?" I would ask. The smile on his face, the twinkle in his eye pleased me..... I just knew he was going to say "sit down etc." But, he didn't. He just stopped what he was doing..... (he was always doing something good)..... and said to me, "What makes your warm breath fog on a cold mirror?" I said I did not know. He replied that I should find out, tell him and maybe, just maybe, I would have a little of my question answered. I walked away disappointed and unhappy cause I didn't get the answer I wanted. Joe always told me, everything. Why not now?? Years passed, and I realized that this was the first time I was shown that I had to start thinking for myself. He really did answer my question, but I did not know it at the time.

Gas Reefer

The little flame went out when we got electricity……… the GAS REEFER went to the garage to be used for storage. The new Westinghouse refrigerator made a loud noise at night….. especially when the compressor kicked in. It also didn't have a little dim blue light that purred. I had to adjust to a new environment. Growing up is really tough. I still don't know why the ice cream stayed cold. A moment in time.

V

"SOW BELLY & BASTED EGGS"

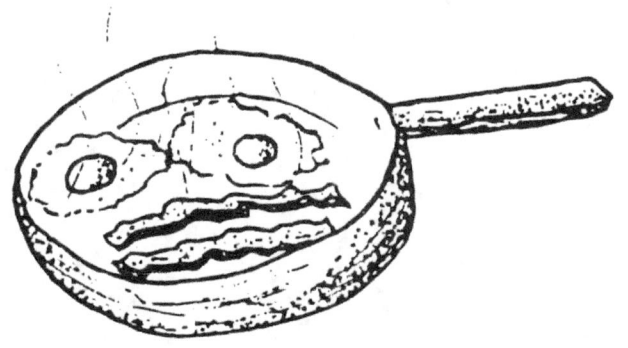

The smell drifted through the house, the screened porch and clear out to the garden. A smell like nothing else in the world..... nothing else even comes close. Some things smell somewhat alike. Like ladies perfumes, or gasoline and kerosene, or pintos vs. navy beans….. but nothing, absolutely nothing in the world smells like my Gram's SOW BELLY & BASTED EGGS.

Generally two times a week she would fix them. More around Hog boiling time. The leaner, thinner and

Sow Belly & Basted Eggs

crispier SOW BELLY the better. Just in case you don't know what this is….. for the city people; SOW BELLY is nothing but un-cured bacon, right off the hog. Some people call it pork belly, fresh pork back, fresh side-pork, or just fresh-side. Nothing like it! BASTED EGGS with just the right amount of water added to the pan made the yolk all white and soft! Joe would smell this from the field, tie the mule up, and come for breakfast. The coffee (I wasn't allowed to have any then) smelled better than it tasted, too! It still does! Gram would then put just the right amount of pepper over the yolk and serve it up with crispy fried, just the right color, thin sliced, fresh potatoes! A breakfast you could kill for!! And, probably would have if I had continued eating <u>like that</u>!

But, at 8-9 years old, who ever thought of diet, or fried in butter foods, or pork fat, or egg yolks and cholesterol. Or, God forbid, a large glass of fresh whole milk, chilled in the reefer so that you almost believed there were ice crystals floating in it!

SOW BELLY & BASTED EGGS………….. Smell is one of the senses, and a powerful one. Think a moment. Every now and again you will remember a pleasant experience through smell. Mostly good thoughts and memories, rarely bad, and I don't know why, but all good pictures come up on the screen. Remember the time you were driving down the highway or street and you smelled BBQ or fried chicken…. just for an <u>instant,</u> that's all it takes, a microsecond.

Sow Belly & Basted Eggs

How about the smell of Jergens lotion? Nothing like it….. or Ivory soap. Just a good clean smell, not adulterated with cheap perfumes or scent. A few things have tenure in our smell-banks and kick in good pictures. You have your own private smell-bank, and so do I. Mine was programed many years ago and the data base that's first on this menu, is SOW BELLY AND BASTED EGGS. Smells and dreams make for good cogitation……..

VI

"MAIL ROUTE"

It was the odd days I believe, as the even days of the week were reserved for home/house/family. The odd days were the "MAIL ROUTE" days for my Grandmother. Gram had worked for the Post Office forever, it seemed to me. I haven't spoken of my Gram as much as the Father figure I had bestowed on my Grandfather the "Saint". Actually, in a young man's eyes my Joe could walk on water….. but what I didn't realize then was that my Gram was invisibly holding him up during this feat!! She was loved as no other Grandmother could be loved.... I just knew this. I cherished her for she was <u>always</u> <u>there,</u> where ever or when ever that was. She took the mail to Oak Grove and Lost Valley on the odd days.

Aguanga, in the mountains some 3,000 feet and located, as the crow flies, some 50 miles due east of San Clemente, CA. Of course, it took hours to get there from anywhere cause the roads curved, and curved and curved again from anywhere to there and back. That's one reason it was nice. Neighbors knew neighbors, and relatives knew relatives. Oak Grove and Lost Valley were "up the road" some 15 miles, a combination of pavement and dirt, up and back. Gram would get in the Sedan, flip the passenger visor down, and her demeanor, stature and position in life changed right before you!! On the inside of the visor (the top of it when in "up" position) there was an official red sign that spelled out, in four inch letters, the words; "U.S. MAIL". She was now an authorized and duly sworn United States Mail Carrier.

Her vehicle was official, and her right to drive on the left side of the road was mandated by Congress and permitted by law. Pulling up to mail boxes to deliver mail through the passenger window was not acceptable nor feasible. She put the mail in the box from her side, while facing traffic (which was stopped for her cause of the sign!). She delivered mail to boxes on the left side of the road going up the hill, and also the left going down the hill. The whole job took some 4-5 hours per day. Her checks came from Washington! I saw

Mail Route

one, one time with an Eagle on it, and knew this was Government stuff and hush- hush!

No body could come near the Official vehicle. As long as that sign was visible, she and the vehicle were untouchable. I used to go on the "MAIL ROUTE" when I did my chores real good or on a special day. Gram had special honks….. some short bursts to warn any evil thing approaching from the other side of the curve that she was coming. Others to let them know she was there so they could meet the official vehicle. Actually, I remember it to be a 1937 Ford two door coupe….. or was it a Chevy?? Regardless, it was official.

Coming home from Oak Grove we could see the home place down in the Valley, and Gram would give one long beep, and two shorts. This was signal to Joe, or any of the relatives down the hill, that she was coming home and would be there in 5 minutes.

When we got home, the sign went back up toward the head-liner part of the car. The transformation took place quickly. Gram didn't look authoritative anymore, she was Gram again, the Invisible Boss. And the apron she always wore went back on and the dark glasses off. Back to reality and unofficial, every day people. It's harder to look official today,,,,, You need a license, a permit, a letter of authorization, a certificate of compliance, a union card, a registration card and more. And you still can't cash a check without a major credit card! I remember the days when all you had to do was flip the visor down, and you had a "MAIL ROUTE". An official

Mail Route

Government Agent of the United States of America. Makes one ponder about progress. Time marches on.

VII

"SPOOKING MULE & SNAKE"

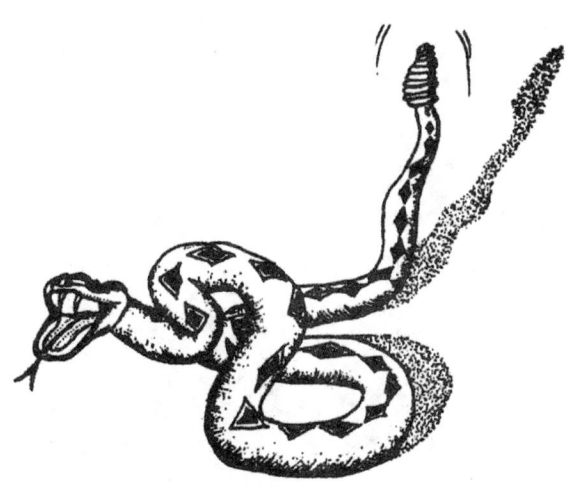

A mule is a mule is a mule. I know, because I used to ride one. Joe had two of them. No tractor then, they were much too expensive. Both mules were for plowing or spring-toothing the row crops. I picked the nicest one (naturally) to ride. Joe said I could ride either one….. and then made a suggestion which one would least likely to buck me off. I picked this one always, as this was the nicest one. No saddle, ride just like the Indians did. I never had a saddle, I've heard that if you put a saddle on a MULE, it will not move forever. It would turn to stone and be there forever and ever. I never did try it.

One beautiful day I set out for the Indian Signal Rock with MULE. Signal rock is visible today from the highway, but you got to know where to look. It's at the top of the mountain behind the home place, above the swamp and right of the hill up from Uncle Dave the hermit's place. If you look real close and good, you can see the space/hole through the rock….. from almost anywhere! But to be there, where the Gods danced, now this was something else again!!

I had been up here often, sometimes that I wasn't supposed to be here. There were secret hiking trails winding through the rocks all the way to the Signal Rock. This was my first time on

MULE. I had a 22 caliber Rising rifle with me, slung over my shoulder and I was "King of the Hill"….. No question about it. I think I was 9 or 10 then and tougher than shoe leather! I played alone a lot, really didn't mind it cause I was used to it. At this point in my life I had no Brothers or Sisters and made do… mostly because I was one tough guy. A few years later I was blessed with a Sister, and then a Brother, and then another Brother….. but that's another story.

MULE had his own way up….. and I let him lead. I knew the hiking trails, but he didn't want to go that way. I wanted to believe I was the boss, but there is a lot to believe about that saying "stubborn as a mule". I don't believe I could have turned him, even if I'd tried. He plodded along, head down and slow

Spooking Mule & Snake

and this was okay with me. I was looking ahead of the trail, hoping I would see a quail or rabbit (as if I could hit it!) for dinner. The next thing I knew MULE had stopped as quick as a wink!! He would not move. I kicked, and kicked and gave the order to "Git up," but to no avail. I was impatient and really slapped and kicked… nothing. So, being tough and smart, I figured a louder noise would do. I pointed the 22 into the air, and pulled off one short… nothing!! He would not move.

I got off, pulled the reins over his head and tried to lead him. <u>Nothing</u>. I climbed back on (not easy without a fence - for a ladder - to climb on first for a 9 year old) and really let him have it with the strongest kick I could muster! MULE moved ahead with a jerk for some ten feet and bucked and made loud noises and scared the bejeebins out of me. I landed on sage brush with gun and canteen flying!! He took off like a greased pig <u>down</u> the hill as fast as he could go. I remember seeing the two rear legs seemingly both in the air all the time. I was more embarrassed than afraid… even though just me and the Gods were the only ones there.

I stood up, feeling more hurt than actual scratches or broken bones. I saw the gun near a rock and headed toward it up the trail. No more than 15 feet in front of me was the biggest diamond back rattle-SNAKE I had ever seen!! Only then did I realize what MULE was trying to tell me with his stubbornness.

The SNAKE, hidden from my view, had SPOOKED MULE!! I felt alone and ashamed. But had to face reality, as no Man in the Hill Country ever left a rattler alive. SNAKE was coiled in the middle of the path. I threw rocks at SNAKE and quickly realized that was stupid as he just coiled tighter and tighter. Rattlers can strike from a coiled position for a distance equal to two times their length. Also they can strike when not coiled (a common mistake made by many a Man with snake fang marks to prove it). My Uncle Harry had told me this, and he was as tough as Joe, but not as Godly. I believed him, so stayed my distance. What to do. Not knowing, I waited and watched. SNAKE did not move, 'cept his tail wagging side to side and the incessant rattle noise kept up. I took time to ponder what I was going to tell Joe about SPOOKING MULE coming home alone.

All of a sudden, SNAKE started to push sand, heading for a rock!! The gun was clear! I ran for it, pointed and pulled off everything she had until chamber was empty. Hurray!!!............ SNAKE was spattered all over the rocks. Much too many bullets had torn him to bits. I ran to him, cut the head off quickly with my Buck pocket knife. Uncle Harry told me they sometimes strike even when cut into pieces….. involuntary something he had said. Then to the prize, the rattles. The skin I had destroyed with the salvo of ammunition, too bad… no belts today. But, WOW!!, thirteen (13) rattles and I cut them off with a swagger typical of the victorious!!

Sitting down after battle, I estimated the length to have been about six feet. Thirteen year old SNAKE huh? I was a hero. Or was I? SPOOKING MULE tried to tell me. He was the smart one. I didn't go to Signal Rock today.

I trotted down the hill, and across in front of the swamp. When home, I told the story with emphasis on my heroics and less on my inability to recognize SPOOKING MULE'S warning signal. Joe and Gram were glad I was not hurt… they had a few words about me having the gun, but still put the rattle in the sun to dry. I dreamed that night of SNAKE and courage. But who really had it?? ….. I know now the SNAKE did, not me, not MULE. He stood his ground, and it was his ground, not mine and certainly not MULES. I was the invader, I was the intruder. I was the evil one with the huge, 4 legged, massive animal and a rider adorned with gun and knife and power….. and I was the winner? I wonder. Little Men growing up learn in most difficult ways. There are more ways than one… live and let live. We all learn by doing, the hard way. Life does pass so very, very swiftly.

VIII

"NETTLES"

Trust is one of the greatest virtues in life. I trusted a couple of my cousins, a little bit. But Joe… now he could ask me to attack the Phoenicians at dawn and I would be up at first light with stick in hand asking which way to battle! No questions asked! Who ever questioned God??

It was in the summer of 1941 and I was getting bigger than my britches, cocky and tougher than nails. I'd be <u>almost</u> 10 next year. (Funny, when you're young, you're "<u>almost</u>," when your old, you are "<u>just</u>"). I had learned to be pulled by a mule with the harness straps burning cross marks into my back behind the plow. I revered Joe when he took the time to show me his scars on his back from the straps crossing in mid back, just below the shoulders. A permanent thing with him. It had taken years to get these marks of a Man. When he got out of Abalone Shell Shower he was snow white everywhere, 'cept his arms and face, and the "V" part under his chin where his shirt was open to the sun. I had never seen such a contrast before. Sort of like he jumped in a big pool of bleach and it got up to his chest, with his arms held high! Never forget it. This was the time he showed me the scars on his back.

We were hunting… well, Joe was hunting, and I was playing "Dog". Ducks would fly in to feed near the irrigation pond that had been made from the dam the Indian had made below the swamp, maybe ¼ mile from the house, toward Indian Signal rock and Hermit Dave's place. Joe was a good shot, naturally, with his side by side Winchester 12 gauge. He had just bagged one flight (the fair way), and it fell almost into the swamp. I took off and tore through the bogs and found the duck….. clean shot! On getting the duck back to Joe, an itch and sting came from my whole left arm. I was complaining and Joe took my arm and said, "NETTLES, huh??" I was careful to avoid this stinging plant, but in the rush to please Joe I had used my left arm to push the "plants" away from my face as I ran into the bogs. I was going to put mud on it as I had seen the Indian do… but Joe told me what to do. He said the oldest and most proven way to quickly

Nettles

rid yourself of NETTLES sting, was to grab some more, crush them in your other hand and rub into the wound real hard.

Now, I was _not_ a kid. I'd been around and killed SNAKE and understood how to get POWER from the SWAMP, and was working on how a GAS REEFER with a flame made things cold… but I just knew that NETTLES _really_ hurt (especially now) and more would just……. make it worse! I thought. But coming from Joe, well, I _had_ to believe him. Not to do so would not only be sacrilegious, but against all history!! So, with some, not much, hesitation I ran back into the bogs, tore some NETTLES off, ran back and proceeded to rub, and rub. Tears came to my eyes, but I rubbed more and more. It hurt so bad I felt like crying, but didn't dare. Then, I heard the Indian and Joe laughing above my silent pain. They both were roaring with laughter. I knew I had been betrayed. My heart hurt so much it seemed like a pain killer to the NETTLES. I ran to the house.

Gram had heard my screaming. She met me on the path outside the screened TREE room. I told her exactly what happened. My crying was almost uncontrollable now, most from the shock that I had been betrayed. She took me in and put some Arm and Hammer paste on the red hot skin and lay me down on the feather bed. I have never seen the Invisible Boss so mad. Joe was walking down the path and I heard the yelling by Gram and swearing by Joe. I closed my eyes and ears to keep out the sound and sight.

Nettles

The next day I learned something profound, a thing I will never, ever forget. Joe came to me in the kitchen, and sat beside me. He apologized for lying to me and said he was sorry. My <u>God,</u> saying <u>he</u> was wrong?? I was not hurt, but surprised that he could do this thing. I never expected Joe to do this, ever. He was my idol, my God and I would have done anything for him. I did not realize he, too, was a human being and could make mistakes. This was an end to the Ideology period in my life. I realize now, Joe could make mistakes, bad ones, and ask forgiveness for his error. I respected him later, much later. For now I removed him from the top of the mount, and let him stroll in life like the rest of us mortals. I would never be the same. A learning experience? Yes……. but something I never wanted to repeat. I knew to trust, but at the same time to be aware that <u>no-one</u> is truly invincible. There is something to that quotation; "To forgive is divine" and I did appreciate that. A memory, a moment, a change in my life.

IX

"SILENT PLACES"

There was one road, and there still is only one road, from Temecula to Aguanga. We never had highway numbers when I was growing up in the mountains. Every one knew exactly how you were going when you said "I'm going to Radec." It is on the road from Aguanga to Temecula, at the junction of the cutoff to Sage. Just as Cahuilla is between Anza and Aguanga. Strange names to some, but not to us. This was all Indian Country and became Spanish Landgrant and Mexican country, long before a good portion of it became what is now called "Rancho California." They call this "progress".

SILENT PLACES are viewed in different form by lots of people. To some, this is a place to escape and collect one's thoughts. To others, its "their room" to sew, cook, read or do nothing. Yet again, it could be a spot at the edge of a meandering stream, or under a TREE at the top of a hill. A place to rest and ponder.

To me there are two SILENT PLACES. Both are off the road between Temecula and Aguanga. Both are quiet, silent and separated from the rest of the world by low, ''private'' looking fences. A ''private fence'' is one that looks private cause of what it keeps inside. One is at the junction of the Sage and Temecula road, a junction called

Radec, some 6-8 miles from the home place. The other is just 3 miles from the house, some 200 feet off the road, and surrounded by a low, black "private fence" with a small, rusted gate. These are the SILENT PLACES where my Gram and Joe are today. They have much Company. My Greatgrand Father, and Grandmother and their children. My Uncle Harry and others I knew or had met.......... at some precious moment in time.

These thoughts are of today, as <u>who</u> <u>ever</u> thought of Death as a Little Man of 8 or 9?? After all, people were supposed to live forever, and the worst tragedy was when your dog was killed. That was something no Little Man wanted to go through again. But, you never thought of God or Invisible Boss not being around. I visit them today, every time I drive from Temecula to the Desert via Aguanga, Cahuilla and Anza. They give me advice now, in a manner softly spoken with quiet repose. These then, are the SILENT PLACES that I remember. Good thoughts… of good people….. forever.

X

"WIRE OF DEATH"

Little Men have heroes….. all Little Men. The heros are not Fathers, or people that you meet at camp or school, but someone that, every time you meet or see them, they have done something that you have never seen or heard of before. Some heroes are in comic strips, such as Buck Rogers or Captain Marvel or Flash Gordon. All heroes of a bygone era. But, in some rare cases, a hero can be an Uncle. This was my case. His name was Uncle Arlie. He was my Gram's brother. Ever hear of a full blooded German Cowboy? That was Arlie.

We used to attend the annual round-up of boy cattle, which always was held at the Bergman stockade just a mile or so above the SWAMP. I would sit on the fence and watch Arlie lasso the little calves, and jump off his horse and tie up the kicking calf! He was a Hero. He could do what Gene Autry and Roy Rogers did in the movies, and what Monty Montana did at the County Fair. Only, this was my Uncle Arlie, my real Uncle, not artificial, but honest to goodness Uncle. I used to play with his children, my cousins, Little Arlie, Esther and Carl (we called him Wogg….. I don't know why). Wogg was older than me, but Esther and Little Arlie were close to me in age and were better at coming down the hill on the wagon. I liked them.

After Uncle Arlie got the calf, he would take it to the fire to be branded, or turn it over and castrate it so it could grow up to be a steer. The good boy calves, (never did determine what made a "good boy calf") were not castrated, but saved and let grow to a big Bull. They made babies and made Uncle Arlie more work, but they made him money I guess. Same thing happened every year.

Uncle Arlie would bring the testicles to Gram, and she would clean 'em real carefully, put 'em in some batter, and deep fry them in lard. This was an annual thing, and all the close relatives came for supper. Rocky mountain oysters they called them. They were delicious. He brought them, My Uncle.

Wire of Death

Arlie used to ride fence, checking for breaks that would let cattle out. He carried, as did Joe, little powerful pliers with WIRE cutters, in a leather pouch on his belt. One day, as in many others like it, he rode down the little hill to Gram and Joe's house for something. Gram and I were standing in the driveway waiting for him. I don't remember what for. He said hello and took something from Gram and rode off toward the west section. We turned to walk to the house, we heard the horse whinny. Something scared the horse. We turned and saw Arlie bucked off, his boot heel was caught in the stirrup. Gram screamed for Wogg and Joe who were nearby. She made me go in the house. When they found him, he was literally cut to ribbons. The horse dragged him for over a mile, through seven barbed WIRE fences. They took Uncle Arlie's

WIRE cutters and cut the barbed WIRE from his body. Joe or Wogg, one of them, shot the horse on the spot. I heard the shot….. I still do.

To this day, when I see a pair of WIRE cutters, I have a moment I can't escape, a bad memory. The WIRE OF DEATH flashes before me. Arlie was gone. He is in the SILENT PLACE with family, and resting well.

XI

"SLAUGHTER HOUSE"

A HOUSE is not a home. I've heard that saying for years, and still don't know where it came from. What I do know is that a SLAUGHTER HOUSE is definitely not a home. Uncle Arlie had one across the main highway from the home place, some 250 yards away from the front grape arbor. The wind was our friend, and almost always blew over the screened "TREE" room toward the highway and not the opposite way.

Slaughter House

SLAUGHTER HOUSE is defined in Webster's dictionary as: "A place where animals are butchered, a place of carnage." Webster also says that carnage is: "Extensive and bloody slaughter; massacre." This was what it was.

Every year, at the time of the round-up at the stockade just a mile up the road, all the cattle chosen for the "HOUSE" would be driven down the road to the HOUSE. They in turn were led into pens that led to chutes (narrow paths to allow one steer at a time), that led to an up-ramp, that led to a loading dock. There was a conveyor belt set up that ran to the left into the big HOUSE.

One must remember, this was (and still is today at many places) a vocation and provided income for Uncle Arlie, and lots of other people who worked for him. Also, he used to "hire out" and sell his services to other cattle ranchers. Much in the same way a cotton gin works, as a co-op. Though this HOUSE was wholly owned by my Uncle Arlie.

I, too, was owned by Uncle Arlie when I worked there. I guess you could call it "owning," as when anybody worked for someone else, they could be fired in those days without recourse. Maybe that was a good thing. I was too young to be concerned about those things. I was lucky to have a part time job to make extra money over my allowance.

There is no use going into details of what happened at the SLAUGHTER HOUSE. It still goes on today, and the pros don't report it in detail either. Killing of anything is not a popular subject, no matter how much one enjoys a good filet mignon or succulent prime rib roast. I did, I do, and that's Okay. What I remember most vividly, is the aura of kindness and quiet tranquility which prevailed just minutes before the death blow was dealt.

All animals were treated with care, washed slowly and pushed gently through the chutes. They were petted and patted and the workers used to whistle soft tunes, quietly and slowly. On my first time, I noticed this and was impressed at the contrast between the atmosphere during the round-up at the stockade with yelling and cheering and the seemingly peaceful, low key presence that prevailed at the HOUSE. Joe was there to answer my question, and answer it he did.

Very directly. It stayed with me for fifty odd years, and that shows it made an impression on me.

He told me as nice as he could, I guess. It seems there is a gland in all animals that makes the meat very tough by releasing some bad stuff….. if they <u>know</u> they are going to die. If they don't know, and are happy and calm, the gland doesn't do anything, and the meat is tender and very tasty. Something called adrenaline.

Up until I got this answer, I used to watch the actual act of killing. All the kids did. My work was inside the HOUSE separating "things" and washing and cleaning. When Joe told me about Happiness and Contentment, I left and went home to ABALONE SHELL shower. I stayed as long as the hot water lasted. I scrubbed and scrubbed and got all the blood off of me, but not the feelings that were deep inside. Many moons passed until these queasy feelings left me. I never went back to the SLAUGHTER HOUSE. There is a fine line between life and death. We are here such a very short time. And time is everything, time cannot be bought or sold, or killed or fired or cleaned or washed. It is precious….. growing up is precious and we do so, so very quickly. Remember?

XII

"COTTONWOOD REUNION"

Family is all encompassing, and ours sure was. With some 400 relatives within 50-75 miles of Aguanga, we just had to have a REUNION every year. Being an 5th generation Californian, I had lots of relatives, lots! It was an annual REUNION and sit down dinner, that lasted two to three days or more. It was a joy. A moment to really reflect.

About 3-4 miles from TREE IN THE HOUSE, across the street from the small SILENT PLACE and less than a mile as the crow flies, is

Cottonwood Reunion

COTTONWOOD REUNION. Uncle Jake lived there, I think. With 400 relatives, it's difficult for a Little Man to remember exactly. But, no difference. All the women made something and brought it.

Not all salads either!! Deviled eggs, scalloped potatoes and vegetables of all kinds, and dips and dips and chips and more chips!! It was a sight to behold. Rows and rows of outdoor slatted tables and benches, with red checked table cloths, lots of ice tea and beer bottles everywhere! All held under the COTTONWOODS. The roads leading in were all cleared, and lined with big rocks on both sides all newly whitewashed and spanky clean. But the highlight was the "pit" barbecue. I have never seen anything like it since.

No little "pit" here. Three days before, the men had dug two deep holes with the benefit of mules and a digger. The digger had a swivel on it and when the mule pulled forward, the shovel part swiveled down, and dug into the ground. This went on until the holes were some four to six feet deep. Now to the good part.

Two days before, the steer had been carefully prepared (I bet they really whistled low and sang soft to this guy!) in preparation for the pit. It was in one piece, clean and shiny. Hundreds of fresh garlic cloves, stuck everywhere. Seasoning sprinkled on, no BBQ sauce at all, ever. Then, what was most impressive, the whole thing was wrapped in parchment paper. That's the crinkly paper that is sort of between wax paper and brown paper bag paper.

Wrapped real good around and tight. Then, very wet "tote" sacks (burlap they call it now) were wrapped around and around until very wet and tight. Then the whole thing was tied with wire and twisted with the pliers/wire cutters until tight, and loose ends cut off.

One giant hog (bout 225 lbs.) was done in the same manner for the second pit. Only difference was, they cut off most of the fat and some of the lean meat <u>before</u> wrapping the hog. This was melted down in huge 10 gallon barrels, boiled and used to fix what the Mexicans call "carnitas" or "little pieces of meat." Very crisp and not greasy cause it was cooked in real hot lard. Carnitas were passed around, with "salsa de cocina" (kitchen hot sauce the <u>real</u> stuff!) to all, while the rest of the meat was cooking in the pits for 36-48 hours.

The same day they prepared the meat, fires had been built inside the pits with oak in one and mesquite in the other, and allowed to burn down to red hot coals. Lots of men lifted the steer and the hog, now fully wrapped and wet, and lowered them carefully into each pit. Steam and hissing noises came from both pits and everyone there shouted satisfaction and success, much like a home-run or touch-down crowd. All men shoveled dirt into the pits covering up everything and stopping the noise and smoke and steam.

Two days later the digging started. Lifting the sacks by a block and tackle mounted over the pits, the meat came out. It was so hot they had to use heavy gloves. Sacks were placed on huge tables and cut open with the pliers/wire cutters and Buck knives. A sight to remember. And the smell. Maybe this could be duplicated in Heaven, no place else!

The scene was always the same; COTTONWOOD feathers drifting in the hot sun, games of horseshoes, baseball and swimmers in the creek. Over 400 bodies, all related and full of joy. Joe, Arlie, Harry, Jake, Wogg, Ray, Dave the hermit, Uncle Frazier, from down below, and men I had never seen performed a miracle for all to enjoy. The knives were sharpened, and slices thick and thin, were cut….. as you liked it!. Lines formed, plates were filled, elation and family ties were assured for another year. Much visiting, loving, caring, security, safety, friendship and tranquility. High point of the year for sure. A time to remember, because it's not that way any more. <u>Nothing</u>

remains the same, <u>except</u> memories and they are good, so very, very exquisitely good.

XIII

"POOLS"

Across the creek from COTTONWOOD REUNION there were the small alluvial plains dropping off from Mt. Palomar. This is the same Mt. Palomar that the world's largest observatory sits on top of. Taking the road from TREE IN THE HOUSE toward the Aguanga store, approximately one mile, you turned left at the store and headed directly to the mountains. There is no road on the east side to get to the Observatory. A big sign is at the end saying Private, No cars, No shooting, and No people." <u>Nobody</u> went in there. A wild man, drunk Indian type that hates kids, was supposed to live there on a land grant he was given many years before. I had seen him only once at the store, and I didn't want to look him in the face. He just looked mad!

Some 3-4 miles from TREE IN THE HOUSE is COTTONWOOD REUNION, and these earthen fans of rocks and sand coming from Palomar Mountain brought with them, moisture, creating the creek we so enjoyed at COTTONWOOD REUNION.

One day my cousin Dickey (who was visiting me from El Segundo) and I decided to walk south from COTTONWOOD REUNION toward the road that hits the mountain across from the Aguanga store. We walked in and out of the creek and it got closer and closer to the mountain as we got near the road. I had always told Joe or Arlie where we were going. This time I hadn't done that.

Pretty soon we came to the dirt road from the store. The big sign was still hanging on a tree. The road turned into a wide path and kept on going right up toward the green trees at the very base of the first hills of the big mountain. As I recall, it was early afternoon, and we were closer to home than when we started, so we decided to turn right and see what was up there. We walked on….. slowly.

About a mile into the small canyon we spotted it. A huge pool at first, a second one up above it a few feet, and a third up higher. Each was built up from the ground, with rocks and cement 3 to 4 feet high, in a perfect circle some

Pools

20 feet across down to 15 feet for the upper smaller one. Three perfect liittle above ground swimming pools, staggered on the edge of this little hill. All were full of crystal clear, ice cold water. At first we thought they were fish ponds, but no fish. Each one had a little waterfall going from one to the other, and the big one's waterfall went into a trough leading to the creek where we had come from. There was a small path leading around to the right of the largest pool.

Now, <u>any</u> <u>body</u> will tell you we had no business there. We knew that, but we just had to look farther and it was not that late. I led the way. We walked up the path to the top pool, and saw a little cement trough 4- 6" deep and 3-4" wide snaking its way up around the manzanita bushes to the mountain. The water in the trough was rushing down into the first little pool. We pushed on. About 10 minutes later we found the source. A BIG Pool at the edge of the BIG mountain fed by a BIG waterfall. It was too much to ignore.

We swam for about five minutes, to the waterfall and back. No one else was to be seen. It was a truly secret place, though we both knew that the mad drunk Indian could show at any time. But he didn't….. until we were heading down the only path to the bottom.

He looked like a Mescalero Apache Indian out of the history books at school!! The kind that scalped first, and yelled later. He had a loin cloth on, and nothing else. We both froze on the path. He walked up to us and just looked….. and looked some more. He had no bow or gun or axe.

Finally, I said something stupid like "Hello."

He glared at me and said, "What are you doing up here, didn't you see the sign??" He said it in perfect English! I just knew he would have a deep Cahuilla dialect, but none came out. Looking like wet rats, Dickey said we had been swimming. The Indian laughed, much to my surprise. He said, "No kidding?" "Do you fellas have a few minutes for a coke?" Well….. this was somethin' else again! We followed him for a few hundred feet to his shack. He lived here by himself and had few friends, he explained. Mostly because people thought he was not friendly. He just wanted his privacy and he loved the outdoors… and he was growing fish after all, but he had just dumped all of them into the creek. He built the POOLS and trough. Seems he was paid by the County of Riverside to grow trout and put them in the creek. His name was Roy Lightcloud and he was a Cahuilla Indian.

We both were invited back to swim, we did and I did several times. We became friends. He ran everywhere, never walking. I would see him at the store sometimes, and I introduced him to Gram. That took some explaining. He taught me a lesson for life. Everyone ignored him, until we became friends. The last time I saw him he was waving good-bye to me after a short swim.

I "broke the ice" so to speak. I will remember him as a kind and happy man….. and I miss him. A friend in my life, a Mad Drunk Indian to most, a true friend to me…………….. Camaraderie for a moment in life, an instant in time.

XIV

"BAGA'S HASH"

The drinking water up at BAGA'S house was much softer than the water at TREE IN THE HOUSE. My Mother and Gram and Aunt Helen and Esther... in fact, all the ladies would come up here to wash their hair. The well was housed in a tall, two story shed with the windmill on the top. It was really in BAGA's front yard. BAGA was my Great Grandmother, she was old when I met her, and seemed the same age when she died some 10 years later.

Baga's Hash

Joe had run a pipe from the tank atop the second story (there for water pressure) down to the first floor and out the wall. The pipe was just sticking out of the wall seven feet high about a foot and had a rope that you pulled and it let water out of the pipe until you let go. There was about a 1" bore of soft, crystal clear, shiny, icy cold water curving out of the pipe….. pouring straight out from the outside wall, following gravity and curving down to splash on your body. It was a happening. Outside with the birds, bees and everything. Nothing ever before has felt this way since. Soap never seemed to wash off cause of the softness, and your hair and body seemed to take on a glisten and be slippery for hours. On a hot day, it was in demand. POOLS were too far away, and we couldn't swim in the reservoir cause of snakes, so this was it! In cold weather, it was back to ABALONE SHELL shower for me. BAGA had an <u>old</u> bathtub in the house.

BAGA would always take left over pork or beef roast and save it in the ice box… made at TREE IN THE HOUSE or wherever, she took it. Remember SMELLS?? Well, the aroma of BAGA'S HASH would hover in the air far from her house. She was up the hill from Little Arlie's (Walt's), which is just up from TREE IN THE HOUSE, stair-step up the hill. <u>Everyone</u> knew when she was making HASH. She would course chop the dry roast, the onions, and the White Rose potatoes and add fresh hand grown sage (which grows everywhere up here) smashed between her palms. The onions had been browned in another pan, and the potatoes and meat cooked until almost

Baga's Hash

crisp in another. All this was put in one big frying pan, add sage, heavy on the pepper and light on the salt, and cover about 1/2 hour on low flame. A minute or two before serving, she would take the top off, turn up the heat and crisp the whole thing. All on a little, bitsy combination gas and wood stove.

People would come for miles. Uncle Harry had a museum up the road east, past the stockade, toward Anza about 5 miles….. And he swore he could smell it up there when the wind came from Palomar Mountain! He sure showed up enough! Everyone used to joke that she should open a cafe serving nothing but BAGA'S HASH and coffee.

I believe that every Great Grandmother would like to be remembered for her tenderness, love, caring, beauty and all the other good things. Most Mothers, Grandmothers and Great Grandmothers do and did possess these things. But BAGA, she is remembered for, <u>not just</u> these things, but for her BAGA'S HASH and icy, cold soft water. What do I think of when I drive by her old house today?? ….. It feels good to remember.

XV

"OLLA CAVES'

Ever since I was a "kid" I've seen clay pots with potted plants. Painted clay pots with fruit in them, pots with handles for water and fancy formed clay pots with "whatever you wanted to put in them" inside. Living in the hill country or really about anywhere in Southern California, we were used to Mexican pots. They were really pretty for a while, then turned more "clay" lookin', and often broke into hundreds of pieces 'cause they would crack easy. Easy come, easy go, 'cause they were cheap and sold everywhere in the Butterfield country.

Yes, the Butterfield Stage….. something like the Pony Express except they had stage coaches with teams of horses. They ran for a few years from St. Louis, Missouri to Oak Grove, California. Lots of stages were lost and many people were killed by Indians. Just look at your re-runs of the Cowboy movies, some are based on truth. But, it is a <u>very</u> <u>true</u> <u>fact</u> that the Butterfield stage came to Oak Grove, about 9 miles from the TREE IN THE HOUSE, east of POOLS. At the turn of the Century and slightly earlier, the stage stations all had Indians selling OLLAS and blankets and stuff they said they found from old relics and ruins.

Uncle Harry didn't ever tell me where he got his OLLAS, but I suspect he got 'em near where I saw them. I knew of two places. Down "below" in the Coachella Valley there used to be an ocean with a shore line and waves crashing on the rocks. The OLLA CAVES were there, at the water line where the Indians took them for water. Left until we found them. Many, many moons ago. Today you can still see the marks of the water line running true to the level for miles Mostly these are in a place called La Quinta, some 30 miles east as the crow flies.

Fake OLLAS were sold lots of places when I was kid, but not the real OYA….. pronounced "Oeeeeyaa," and spelled the Indian/Spanish way; "OLLA." They were in peoples' yards in sort of protected areas with little fences and vines planted either in them or around them. They, too, were taken for granted when I was young, but not today.

On visits to Indian Signal Rock (without MULE), I found a few caves just walking around. Mostly looking for snake pits….. where snakes live. They love caves, cause they are warm, dark, quiet, and private. A safe haven for snakes….. until I found them! Little Men do strange things, and I did, and I wasn't alone.

Remember Uncle Harry had plenty of OLLAS in his museum, inside and out. They were really part of his landscape. All different shapes and from various tribes that only Uncle Harry could tell. Some had old, very old, designs on them with faded paint. He treasured most of them. Me and some other guys found the OLLAS in the hills. We found them at the water line down "below," and we found them near INDIAN SIGNAL ROCK. We scared the snakes off. We did bad things….. we broke some of them, <u>on purpose.</u> What do Little Men know of antiquity? We were to blame, but it was not thought of as bad then, as we know it to be now.

A moment of history, gone in an instant. Bad memories for me and the others, I'm sure. History destroyed by young Little Men who knew not what they were doing. Forgiveness by the GODS of INDIAN SIGNAL ROCK and those of down "below" have been requested silently for many years. Were our apologetic voices of humility and shame heard? Will we ever know???.....
... Growing up so fast, so quickly…… regretful moments…… in time.

XVI

"PIÑON FLATS"

There is a flat area some 25 miles east of TREE IN THE HOUSE at approx. 1500 feet altitude with a nice view of the valley "below". This is on the road to Coachella Valley and it takes about 45 minutes because of the winding road. At this altitude pine trees are lucky to grow, and those are scrub pines mixed with ocotillo plants and a few yucca and manzanita. For some unknown reason, the little pine trees here produce small pine cones that are filled with PIÑONS! PIÑON means pine-nut or pine kernel in Spanish (with a little curl over the first "N") and flat is <u>flat</u> and in English that's: "smooth and regular on the horizontal with little or no slope." PIÑON FLATS…….. full of all good memories, no bad ones, and my SMELL-BANK is really in gear when I get near PIÑON FLATS. What did your screen pull up in its SMELLBANK the last time you drove through some pine trees?? Smell…….. what I mean? Good, clean, fresh, crisp and invigorating…… Right??

This was a perfect place for a picnic. If the Gods ever designed a place just for picnics, this would be it! On more than a few occasions, Gram would drive the un-official mail car to PIÑON FLATS and meet friends and family, who lived below, at this halfway meeting place. It had all anyone needed for a picnic. Tables, out-houses, room to play and room to hide, trees to climb and manzanita bushes to make slingshots out of to shoot little pine nuts at each other.

The pine nuts made good ammunition as they were the right size for the sling-shot pad and didn't <u>really</u> hurt when you got hit! This was the only ammunition I knew of that you could eat after you got shot! PIÑON nuts you crack, like a little peanut, and eat the delicious white meat inside. Trouble was, you had to get there before the squirrels did, as they were faster and better at shelling than we were! At the right time of year there were lots of pine cones to break apart and a feast would be had by all.

The WPA (Works Progress Administration) built the tables and outhouses about 1933- 38 and they were maintained till a few years ago. They built the road too, and the gutters along the side of the road. Little flat rocks cemented together to keep water flowing down hill and so as not to cut a stream across the road when we had a "gully washer." Today you can still see some of this edge work near the bottom of the PINES TO PALMS road. This is the road that PIÑON FLATS is on……… My PIÑON FLATS.

After a picnic, all would be full, tired, and happy. Both the folks from "down below" and from TREE IN THE HOUSE would leave feeling blessed with good family and felt fortunate to be so close….. in both location… and in heart. The drive to Aguanga via Anza and Cahuilla was short and always a little sad and happy at the same time.

Sad….. that it was over, but happy that we knew we would see each other again.

I looked forward to the picnics at PIÑON FLATS….. I can't remember the last picnic I was on….. Why don't we have more picnics today?..... Why does growing up mean less picnics?..... It shouldn't……… When was the last picnic you were on???????????? Everyone should make more time for "picnics".

The good times, the lasting times, the memorable times……………. the forever times.

XVII

"ISINGLASS SLIDE"

Down "below" generally meant to Coachella Valley. This was about 55 miles as the crow flies, an hour and 1/2 minimum driving due to the crooked road down the "PINES TO PALMS" route. From TREE IN THE HOUSE, to Uncle Harry's museum, to Cahuilla and Anza, over the Cleveland grade to another road where you turned right, went right past PIÑON FLATS and down to below sea level in the Valley. This was <u>really</u> desert. Down "below" also meant to Hemet and San

Isinglass Slide

Jacinto where JOE took the corn, tomatoes and other vegetables to market. But, normally it meant to Coachella Valley.

The Valley was not like Aguanga at all. It was "flat" farming country and seemed dusty and hot all the time. But a lot of people lived there cause it was easier to farm and they had lots of water and much warmer weather. I didn't know it then, but I was going to live there some day… soon….. and for a long, long time.

I made some friends near COTTONWOOD REUNION, POOLS, TREE IN THE HOUSE, and SILENT PLACES. Little Arlie (Walter) and some of the other guys took a trip one weekend to a place like an oasis in the middle of the Sahara desert. It was about ten miles north of the city of Indio, way back in the Chocolate Mountain range. An older guy who knew this place had talked to Gram and Joe 'bout me going. It was okay.

We arrived at dusk. The leader had wanted to go further into the canyon, but he got stuck. It was an old panel truck and we all pushed, and pushed. But, this was it. This is where we were destined to camp. With tarantulas, scorpions, snakes, lizards and whatever else was here, we really had to be careful. No trees to put our hammock in so we could get off the ground. The brave ones slept on the ground, the chickens in the back of the truck. I started on the ground, sneaked onto the bed of the truck much later, and at dawn crawled quietly back to my rocky bed. No one ever knew that I really was a chicken.

Isinglass Slide

In the morning we saw a sight!! The "Valley" was downhill behind us, green and pretty. In front of us was the worse looking brown, ugly hills I had ever seen. Off to the right about a mile was a bunch of palm trees and a little further on some more bunches of palms. The leader said one was Curtis Palms, and the other called Biskra Palms. We were going to explore both today. After breakfast, we doused the fire (never could figure out why... rocks don't burn!), and took off. In about half an hour we were standing in one oasis of the desert as described to me earlier. The trees were all Washingtonia Palms, huge, green and majestic..... like they were guarding this place from the evil ones! There was water, salty though, but it looked just like the place that Errol Flynn would stand and fight when he was defending his damsel in distress! We all played doing what 8-9 year old Little Men do to make themselves believe they are heroes. It was fun, but short lived. We needed more excitement.

The leader said we could do some exploring, but to be back at a certain time. I remember him putting his hammock between two palm trees..... he was going to sleep. We took off.

A magic place it was..... and I have been unable to find it since. We were "marching" along the top of a ridge, and saw from above, the beautiful colors of large mounds of what looked to be sand. They were some 150 to 200 feet down at the bottom of this hill, which was in a canyon about an hour's walk from the camp. The surface of the side of the hill we were walking on was shiny and slick. Being Little Men and curious, we

Isinglass Slide

investigated further. One guy sat down on top of the hill, with his legs pointing down hill and took off like a greased pig!! He slid into a puff of dust at the bottom! We all thought he was dead for sure!! When the dust cleared, he popped up smiling with blue and pink dust all over him. So….. nothing more need be said. For the whole afternoon we slid and slid and slid. Into different colors of the powder. Powder like ladies use on their faces, dust, fine and smooth like chalk; powder puff like stuff!! One guy went to get the leader to show him. They came back and he was amazed. This was a natural phenomenon and looked like no one had ever been here. He said it was ISINGLASS….. None of us ever heard of it.

Later we found out we had been sliding on a bed of Mica, (Isinglass) created by Mother Nature. Different colors of mica, that came off in large sheets that were transparent. An ISINGLASS slide… we created a slide that was concave and became more molded to our bodies and created even more powder as we slid down.

Back at TREE IN THE HOUSE, I shared my "find" with Joe and Gram. Joe showed me, something. A new stove he bought for Gram. It had an ISINGLASS window in the door of the oven that didn't break with the heat.

I knew what ISINGLASS was at 9. I knew what, why and when it was used, and I had my own supply! I was proud that I knew. What I didn't know was that tempered glass had just been invented and replaced Mica. I'm glad I didn't know. I tried on several hikes in the years to come to find this secret place. Never did. I know it's there, I see

Isinglass Slide

the slides, I know the colors of the powder and the screams of the guys and I see the smiles on the faces and hear the yells of joy….. but, it is gone from my life now, and only a memory. Will it be found? I <u>know</u> it will be ….. in my mind. It's there, and so am I………………….. A moment of fun, a time of growing and pure pleasure, sunshine and….. Little Men growing up fast….. very, very fast.

XVIII

"PINES TO PALMS"

Or you may say, "PALMS TO PINES," it depends on if you're going up or coming down! This road gives you one of the most beautiful views in the world. It runs from the high mountain cities of Idlewild and Mountain Center thru to join the road from TEMECULA, AGUANGA, CAHUILLA and ANZA. It passes PIÑON FLATS, SANTA ROSA CUTOFF, LITTLE SUGAR LOAF MOUNTAIN, BIGHORN OVERLOOK, SALTON SEA POINT and other pretty places you….. or someone else, can name. It runs from approximately 5000 feet to below sea level in Thermal, California. We went "down below" often, and I didn't enjoy many trips.

Joe was a full blooded Frenchman, tall and powerful. His last name was SALLEE, and his full name was JOSEPH WARDER SALLEE, (pronounced "Sal-lay"). Gram thought he was good lookin', I didn't know. Gram was a full blooded German lady whose name used to be BERGMAN before marrying Joe. Sometimes the French and German really had words over some things. They really got mad sometimes, and Joe always thought he won, but I knew different! The Invisible Boss always seemed to get her way even though Joe got in the last word!

Joe used to drive fast. I was always in the back seat moving from side to side, trying to hold on. No need to tell you anymore. Gram would have to tell Joe to stop for a minute for me to get some fresh air. The car sickness had come over me. Usually I could make it to SALTON SEA point, but not always. Often, I "lost," my lunch. My memory of travel actually going down is not a pleasant one. But, each trip was worth it when we got there.

I had a Mother. It's very rare you find a Little Man who does not. Mine was always available when I needed her. She had the best of the French and the best of the German. She was beautiful and soft, yet strong and forceful and seemed to usually get her way, like Gram. She would visit me at TREE IN THE HOUSE, we would go together to SILENT PLACES and BAGAS and she often visited us at PIÑON FLATS. Mother worked as a divorced/single woman in Hollywood in the theater with people such as Xavier Cugat and many others. She was a dancer and singer at the Paris Inn and other places. I always heard she was good, from her Mother, Gram, but didn't really know <u>how</u> <u>good</u> until much later in my life. She and my "real" Father were divorced before I could walk and they are not subjects of this story. In later years I was blessed to get a <u>second</u> Father, and then a <u>real</u> Sister, and a Brother, and another Brother. But, that's another story............. another period in my life and I shall tell you someday. Another time, another book, another chapter in my life. Living has been good to me. I will continue............***in time!***

FINIS

❧ AUTHOR'S NOTE ☙

Thank you for taking a little bit of your life to read about a mini-part of mine.

This has been but a small segment of my life………. so please, always remember, it's not the length of life that's important, but its contents!

Laguna Beach, California
March 11, 1992

www.ingramcontent.com/pod-product-compliance
Lightning Source LLC
LaVergne TN
LVHW021330080526
838202LV00003B/121